Chinese Astrology

Chinese Astrology

THE KEY TO UNDERSTANDING YOURSELF

MASTER KAY TOM CH DS YHH

SIRIUS

SIRIUS

This edition published in 2023 by Sirius Publishing, a division of
Arcturus Publishing Limited,
26/27 Bickels Yard, 151–153 Bermondsey Street,
London SE1 3HA

ISBN: 978-1-3988-3028-8
AD010728US

Printed in China

CONTENTS

If you don't
understand your life,
you won't understand if
you are a good person.

CONFUCIUS
551-479BCE

DEDICATION

I would like to dedicate this book to my Chinese master of
over 25 years, Grand Master Chan Kun Wah and the Chue Feng
Shui Foundation Lineage, in thanks for their total commitment to
furthering the wisdom of the ancient Chinese philosophy of
Feng Shui and Chinese horoscope to the benefit of mankind,
and for enriching the quality of my own life beyond measure
through their wise words.

I would also like to include in this dedication my own family—my
son Nick, my daughter Carrie, their spouses Liv and Brett, and my
beautiful grandchildren Tilly, Jemima, Delphine, and Quinn—for
their love and support, and with grateful thanks for ensuring the
continuity of my own genes.

Kay Tom
FENG SHUI MASTER

MASTER KAY TOM CH DS YHH
CHAIRMAN OF THE CHUE FOUNDATION

To know how to connect to energy
is to know how to seize good
opportunities and avoid the bad,
just as a wise fisherman knows
exactly when to cast his net.

FOREWORD

SHINE BRIGHT
LIKE A DIAMOND

A diamond is recognized and respected for the radiance of its multifaceted brilliance and for its natural ability to shine. This hasn't always been the case, and most certainly is not a given, since the diamond has endured a long journey of evolution through intense pressures underground before it is mined from the bowels of the earth in all its glory. Such is the magnitude of the journey, and subsequent extraction from the earth, that diamonds are deemed precious and carry the honor of being the hardest material on earth.

Chinese astrology helps you find your own inner diamond, to encourage you on your journey through the kaleidoscope of life, and to enable you to shine in your own unique way. Everyone has a gift, and this is the tool to help you to identify that gift, that unique quality that resides inside you. There is no judgment, no less or more, no better or worse, and no higher or lower. In life, we set our own bar to suit our needs, our skills and ourselves.

THE POWER OF THE ROOT

This beginner's guide to Chinese astrology builds a solid foundation to the subject by ensuring a strong root through the understanding of the origins of this ancient philosophy. A solid foundation that is built slowly encourages the longevity and validity of the knowledge, and a strong root guarantees a strength that will hold firm in any storm or challenge that may cross your path.

A strong root will hold you firm, no matter the strength of the storm, ensuring the fruits of your labor will be of benefit for years to come. Chinese astrology comes from a strong root that is both tried and tested.

My aim in this book is to illustrate the validity of this ancient philosophy and the immense benefit of a deeper understanding of the self—and, moreover, your connection to the most powerful commodity of all: Mother Nature. To play to your strengths can only be beneficial; to know your weaknesses is to avoid pitfalls.Strategy is the key to success; anticipation and preparation are close allies.

Chinese astrology enables you to change your perspective on life and the world around you. In this era of a heightened awareness of the needs of nature, there can be no better time to deepen your understanding of the language of nature to support her sustainability. It is abundantly clear that nature isn't happy, and needs our attention and care. That can be done through understanding the principles of Chinese astrology and Feng Shui. Respect is the priority.

As you read these pages, it will become more and more apparent that this is a deep and intricate subject with an array of twists and turns that necessitate a very logical brain. If you like patterns and formulas, and have a deep respect for nature, this subject will resonate with you. It must be said that this book is just a basic learning tool; primarily, it is an introduction to the concept and the potential of this deep and intricate subject.

Indeed, it is the unique quality of Chue Style Feng Shui that I represent, for no knowledge has ever been taught from a book but has always been transmitted by the direct word of a master to avoid any misinterpretation or misinformation. This is the purity and the quality of Chue Style Feng Shui. It is my privilege to be part of the Chue journey, with a lineage that dates back many generations, through the imperial courts of China.

Master Kay Tom CH DS YHH

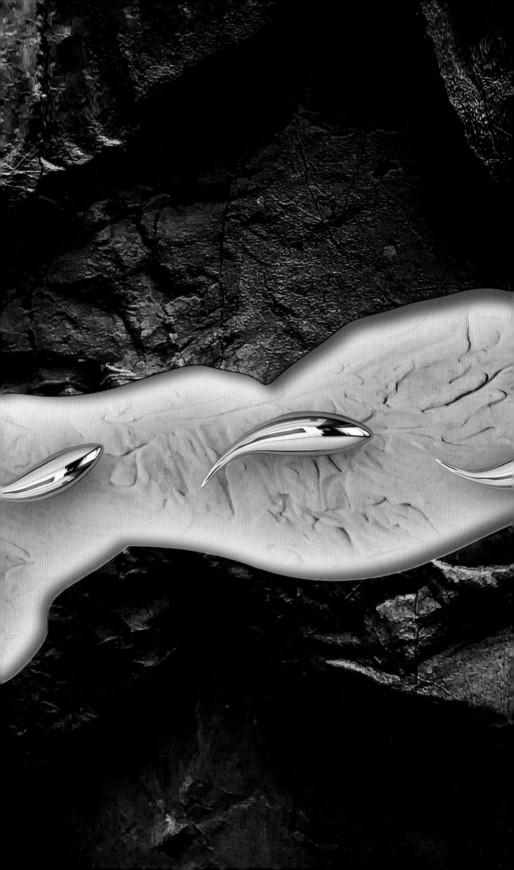

Chapter 1

THE LEGACY OF CHINESE ASTROLOGY

T he wisdom and understanding of the ancient Eastern philosophy of Chinese astrology date back more than 3,000 years, illustrating how the principles of this deep-rooted subject have stood the test of time with a strength and validity that is still recognized and valued.

The wise elders and masters of the imperial courts of China have labored through many Chinese dynasties, from one generation to the next, to understand the intricacies of the knowledge that 100% translates into the language of nature. Each generation has added its own layer of understanding through direct research on the effects of the application of this knowledge on humanity.

There is no greater power than that of nature, and there certainly is no denying who the boss is. Nature dictates everything from a light, refreshing rainfall after a period of intense heat to the affront of a tsunami on the shores of an ocean, and everything in between. No one can deny her magnificence and her fortitude. Therefore, it makes perfect sense to listen to her wisdom, follow her wise example and, of course, have her on your team.

Chinese astrology is a tool for tapping into the guidance of nature's wisdom by identifying the energy of nature that is encountered at the very moment a baby takes its first breath. This is the first experience of life on earth for the baby, and first impressions count. Understanding the energetic values present at a birth helps us understand that baby's energetic DNA; it is in effect an X-ray of the baby's genes.

Genes are a significant factor in how the baby will develop into his own person. Physically, we witness the continuity of a gene when we recognize family traits and likenesses, in both appearances and mannerisms, that are passed from one generation to the next. For example, it is often the case that a family that earns its living through the arts will produce artistic children. On my morning walk through the beautiful English countryside, I recently met a Border Collie named Monty and his owner. After exchanging brief pleasantries, I continued with my journey only to realize quite quickly that Monty had changed direction, and had joined me. He raced ahead to the gate that led into the next field and was guarding the area. His owner explained that this was a habit from birth. Border Collies are working dogs who usually live in a farming environment and support the farmer by controlling a herd of sheep and assisting in their movement from one field to another. Monty had treated me as he would one of his sheep, and was barking at the gate to stamp his authority. There most certainly was no aggression toward me. Monty lives in a domestic setting, but his gene has not forgotten his true nature.

The information gained through Chinese astrology gives a deeper layer of understanding of a person's makeup and totally explains their character. We are all individuals with different skills, different priorities, different backgrounds, and different opportunities, and there are no hard and fast rules to life. There is no judgment about who is better and who is worse; we are who we are, and we are governed by our energetic DNA. Acceptance and understanding are the keys; then there is no sibling rivalry or peer pressure or any of the multitude of expectations that can be thrown our way.

Chinese astrology offers the gift of understanding the strengths and weaknesses of an individual and where his direction lies. The headmaster at my son's school once said to me, "Our endeavor is to make each child shine—be it in the classroom, the science laboratory, on the sports field or in the woodwork shop. Every child has a gift."

Chinese astrology is the tool to identify that gift. Chinese astrology helps us understand the self, mine our own inner diamond, and, of course, encourage it to shine.

Chapter

2

THE WISDOM OF NATURE

M an's reliance on nature became more than apparent during the lockdowns imposed due to the pandemic and subsequent health crisis in 2020/21. The first sector to bounce back to life when the restrictions were lifted was the property market, where real-estate agents were experiencing an unprecedented demand for houses in the countryside, or those with a back yard. Such was the extent of the realization of our need for nature. Life-force energy is the commodity gifted to us by nature and the environment we live in. A good supply of this powerful resource is as vital to our well-being as the purity of the air we breathe. This was a deprivation during those long periods of lockdown, and so desperate was the need to replenish it, as soon as the tiniest ray of light appeared in the opening of the door of release, people flooded to the countryside and beaches in a desperate attempt to get their fix. To take time out in nature is to clear the mind—a vital aspect for our well-being in this modern world, which operates at a fast

pace and pushes our mental health to its limit. Test it for yourself when challenges present themselves by making the space to walk in the peace of a forest or somewhere similar and to witness how the highway mayhem that fills your mind suddenly has a different perspective, and how the answers can consequently show themselves to you. The truth of the matter is that there is tremendous peace that resides in all of us if we make the time to find it. I recently heard a lady with a passion for her garden say, "The garden is where I go when I want to lose myself to find myself." Such is man's connection to nature.

The life-force energy that nature provides is all around us in greater or lesser degrees. To test this, consider your level of fatigue after a day spent in a shopping mall in a busy city compared to a day spent hiking in the mountains with only flora and fauna for company. The city contains far more people needing to share the valuable life-force energy that a few parks and rivers can provide compared to the space of the countryside, especially the mountains, where the air is purer and there's a lot more energy to go around. The trees, bushes, vegetation, grass, flowers, countryside, mountains, and oceans all produce this valuable commodity that brings life to all it encounters. Gifted people can physically see this energy in their surroundings,

energy that is known as *chi*. Those who can't see it can certainly see evidence of it in the vibrant foliage in their environment. Research this for yourself by planting identical bulbs in different locations in your yard and see which comes up first. The first will always come from the area of earth with the best energy—energy that is warm beneath the ground and has used this support on its journey of germination through the winter months. Observing your surroundings, note how in areas where the ground is warmer snow will always melt quickly; conversely, in areas where the layer of snow is more prolonged, the ground is cold and there is no energy.

All living creatures understand energy—especially animals, birds, insects, and sea life. To simply observe the habits of these creatures is to witness their respect for nature. The elephants of Sri Lanka acted out of character on the day before the tsunami of the Indian Ocean in 2004 hit its shores. The local people could not understand it when the elephants lifted the village children onto their backs and carried them to a higher position on the mountain. The elephants knew there was a change in the energy of the land.

Following nature's guidance allows us to make the connection, and to harness and utilize her strength. By following her example, we are encouraging the best possible flow to our daily life, be it in the workplace, at school, or in the home. Projects can progress, concentration can be heightened, and family life is harmonious.

A time to reap—a time to sow.
A time to work—a time to play.
A time to act—and a time to withdraw.
A time to run and a time to walk.

Birds sing their dawn chorus with the rising sun because they know this is the freshest and most valuable energy of the day. They give birth to their young in the spring because they know this is the freshest energy of the year. A hedgehog is nocturnal, and will hunt at night because it primarily uses its senses of hearing and smell, and nighttime is when the environment is quieter. Birds and animals play to their strengths.

Using nature's advice through the information offered in a Chinese astrology reading helps us understand all of the above and play to our strengths. To go against nature is a poor decision; it can have unfortunate consequences when life becomes hard and fatigue is an issue. The power of a Chinese astrology reading is to identify where your strengths lie as well as your vulnerabilities, for to know your enemy is to expose him and to know where he sits means to negate the chance of him catching you unaware. The reality of life is that the vulnerabilities are there, and not everyone is as honest and open as you are. So take off the rose-tinted spectacles that only allow you to see the good in others, wise up to the truth of the matter, and protect yourself. Knowing your enemy enables you to do this.

To know how to connect to energy is to know how to seize good opportunities and avoid the bad, just as a wise fisherman knows exactly when to cast his net.

Chapter

3

THE TIDE ALWAYS RETURNS

To understand cycles is to bring a confidence and a peace
of mind that comes from the reliability of that cycle and
the subsequent guarantees in life that it represents.
Imagine standing on a shore, looking out to sea, and witnessing
a place where the beach has been laid bare as the tide is out,
the boats are lying marooned, and the mussels are motionless,
clinging to the bare rocks and basking in the sunshine, quietly
accepting their fate. However, all is not lost; we know the tide will
return, the boats will sail, and the mussels will dance, bringing
the scene back to life once again. This reminds us that no matter
how dire a situation may feel, things change and life returns. Such
is the reliability of nature and the cycles she represents, cycles
representing continuity that in turn give a feeling of security. This
is the gift of nature.

The power of the principle of continuity was illustrated very
clearly on the passing of the most amazing monarch of all time,
Queen Elizabeth II. She had reigned for more than 70 years

and her people in the UK, the Commonwealth, and around the world had come to rely on her steadfast support and guidance. Undeniably, this lady had dedicated her whole life to her cause, and on her passing the outpouring of deep admiration and affection was palpable. To many, Queen Elizabeth was a rock to cling to, and represented the security that continuity brings. Chinese astrology is based on the continuity of the solar cycle and the lunar cycle.

THE NATIONAL STADIUM, BEIJING: THE BIRD'S NEST
THE PEACE OF MIND THAT COMES FROM THE CONTINUITY OF NATURE'S CYCLES

The most natural place for a bird to fly when it encounters a problem is to the security of the family nest. This thinking can be

applied to the creation of the National Stadium in Beijing when it was designed to host the 2008 Summer Olympics. It was here that a record number of athletes broke their previous personal best times, and spectators experienced comfortable seating and good views of the proceedings. Everyone felt at home, illustrating humans' reliability on, and connection to, their environment and the support that the cycles of nature bring.

THE SOLAR CYCLE
THE 24 HOURS OF THE DAY

The sun represents the fire energy that provides light to sustain all forms of life. Without light, vegetation would not grow and humans would be without food.

North	No sun	Midnight
East	Rising sun	Early morning
South	The height of the sun	Midday
West	Setting sun	Late evening

The sun rises in the east, making this the freshest and most active energy of the day. To rise early is to embrace this quality with a fresh mind and clear thoughts that help us address the commitments of the day ahead.

The fullness of the sun shows in the south at midday. This is when activities are at their peak and people are very busy. This is also the time when energy starts to decline, because people have reached their limit. To continue in the afternoon at the same pace as the morning is to encourage fatigue to set in quickly, as this action is going against nature's example.

As the sun heads west, its energy grows quieter. This is evening, when the family is returning home after their busy day, and they're eager to gather around the dinner table to share good food and their experiences of the day. The western position is receiving the energy of the sun as it goes down, and is storing the energy.

Now the sun is beneath the horizon and the earth is dark. This is a natural time to rest and restore; the human body is like a battery that needs to be recharged. Our vital organs begin their healing process during the night too, so it's important to get a good night's sleep.

THE LUNAR CYCLE
THE 28-DAY CYCLE OF THE MOON

Seventy percent of the earth is covered in water, and the moon controls its movement to such an extent that we can buy a timetable from any coastguard's office and identify to the minute the times of high and low tide each day. The human body is also 70% water, and the female menstrual cycle is connected to the 28-day cycle of the moon, once again illustrating the human connection and reliance on nature, as water is the staff of life.

THE CYCLE OF THE FOUR SEASONS
THE AGRICULTURAL CYCLE AND THE MIRACLE OF THE SEED

Each season has its own responsibility. The three months of each offer a beginning, a middle, and an end to the journey of the chi.

 **SPRING:** The birth of the energy when we witness new life in the form of buds on the trees and life returning after the rigors of the restrictions of winter. The direction represented here is the **EAST**, where the sun rises.

 **SUMMER:** The height of the energy when trees are in full bloom and people are full of life, enjoying warmth and outdoor activities. The direction represented here is **SOUTH** and the height of the sun.

 **FALL:** Energy starts to descend and the leaves fall from trees, beginning the journey of the recycling of the chi as the nutrients from the leaves are absorbed into its roots. The direction represented here is **WEST**, as the setting sun is receiving the energy.

 **WINTER:** Germination is taking place in the warmth of the earth, where the seed will rest until the weather is warmer and the cycle can begin again in the spring. The direction represented here is **NORTH**, where there is no sun.

THE CYCLE OF THE 12 MONTHS OF THE YEAR

Each of the four seasons represents three months; 12 months give a deeper understanding of the movement of the energy throughout a year. Each month has its own character and its own responsibility in ensuring the continuity of the cycle. The movement of the energy throughout the year can be likened to a relay race where the baton of responsibility in carrying the chi forward is passed from one month to the next as the year progresses. In Chapter 5, we take a deeper look into this journey through the 12 animals of the Chinese zodiac and the 12 months of the year.

These are the cycles of nature that ensure with confidence a continuity for us all to rely on.

Chapter

4

THE
LANGUAGE
OF NATURE

HEAVEN, 天
EARTH, 地
HUMAN 人
CHI 氣

Chinese philosophy is based entirely on the power of three, being the three dominant energies of life: Heaven, Earth, and Human Chi. Heaven Chi represents Heaven's will and what a person is born with; Earth Chi represents the planet Earth and the impact of the environment on the life of humans; and Human Chi represents Man, who transmits and transmutes these two powerful energies, bringing them together. A birth chart is constructed on a representation of these three energies.

THE BASIS OF A BIRTH CHART

TIME OF BIRTH	DAY OF BIRTH	MONTH OF BIRTH	YEAR OF BIRTH
Human Chi	Human Chi	Human Chi	Human Chi
Heaven's Chi	Heaven's Chi	Heaven's Chi	Heaven's Chi
Earth's Chi	Earth's Chi	Earth's Chi	Earth's Chi

Every year, month, day, and hour carries a representation of the energy of Heaven and the energy of Earth at any given moment.

BA ZI 八字 THE FOUR PILLARS OF DESTINY

Chinese astrology is also known as *Ba Zi*, which means "eight characters." A birth chart comprises four columns, known as the Four Pillars of Destiny, that are based on the year, month, day, and hour of a person's birth. Each column has a representation of Heaven and Earth energy that was present at the time of birth, and affords a consultant the opportunity to address the balance between these two powerful commodities. Four columns x two energies give us the eight characters of the Ba Zi.

The eight characters of the Ba Zi chart represent the life of a person: their natural behavior and particularly their behavior within the four seasons. Collectively, these eight characters are the blueprint of a person's energetic DNA, which encourage and guide them along their life path. All you have, all that you are, and

all that you will be are there from the moment of the first breath. Each of the eight characters of a chart are represented by one of the five elements from the cycle of the five elements. Through the understanding of the characteristics and interactions of these elements comes the understanding of the energy nature is conveying and the interpretation of a chart.

A BIRTH CHART

HUMAN CHI	TIME 06:00	DAY 4th SELF	MONTH July	YEAR 2022
HEAVEN CHI	Yin Wood	Yang Earth	Yang Fire	Yang Water
EARTH CHI	Yin Wood	Yang Fire	Yang Fire	Yang Wood

The Heaven energy present on the day of birth is the foundation stone of a reading, as it represents the **self**. In the example above, the person born on July 4th 2022 at 06:00 hours carries the characteristics of the self-element of Yang Earth, with which the other seven characters of the chart react. To interpret the interaction of these elements, we need to understand the characteristics of the five elements and also the Law of the Five Elements.

THE LAW OF THE FIVE ELEMENTS

To further interpret what nature is communicating, it is important to study the Law of the Five Elements.

THE SUPPORTING CYCLE

Wood fuels the **Fire** to make it burn.

Fire burns to form an ash that is deposited on the **Earth**.

Earth is where **Metal** is extracted.

Metal when melted forms a liquid, which is akin to **Water**.

Water feeds **Wood** and encourages its growth.

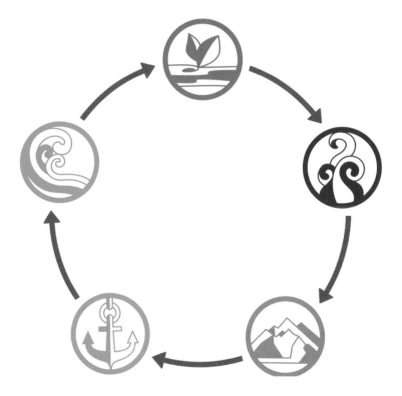

Looking back at the birth chart, July 4th 2022, 06:00, on the previous page, we observe that the self-element Yang Earth has

three aspects of Yang Fire present in the chart to support the Yang Earth. There are also three Wood elements to support the Fire and one Water to feed the Wood; therefore everything is feeding into the self.

The challenge for the chart is that there is no Metal element present; therefore there is a break in the flow of energy. This can manifest as someone who doesn't do anything for himself; everything feeds into him, and then he doesn't produce anything himself. According to the Law of the Five Elements, his self-element of Earth doesn't produce the Metal.

THE CONTROLLING CYCLE

Wood controls **Earth** as the roots of the tree penetrate the Earth.
Fire melts **Metal** when the heat intensifies.
Earth controls **Water** by giving it direction through the banks of the river.
Metal controls **Wood** when the metal axe chops the wood.
Water controls **Fire** and can put out a fire.

Looking at the Controlling Cycle of the Law of the Five Elements, we can see the same chart has three Wood present to control the self. In this case, that isn't a bad thing, as the self-element of Earth can be stubborn when it is so strong (with all other elements feeding into the self on the Supporting Cycle in this example). So the roots of the tree penetrating the Earth will break

it down to allow for the absorption of water to encourage the Earth to produce something.

Every chart tells a story, a story that is interpreted through the interaction of the elements present in the chart. When there is an element missing, it is hard for that person to identify or connect to that element. One client came to me when she failed her driving test eight times. Looking at her birth chart, I identified the fact that she had no Metal element in the chart; the car represented the Metal element. On this occasion, I used Feng Shui on her home to support the Metal element; we also chose a day that represented Metal for her next appointment, and she passed her driving test on her ninth try. However, she never enjoyed driving, because the Metal element was never a part of her DNA.

THE FIVE ELEMENTS

Reading and interpreting a birth chart is like digitally editing a photograph by adjusting the exposure, white balance, levels, and the numerous layers that can be applied. In the same vein, we can gain further clarity of a chart when we consider the yin and yang aspects of an element.

YANG WOOD

This is a strong, mature wood such as that of a large tree.

YIN WOOD

This is a softer, more gentle wood, such as the new shoots emerging from the ground, small shrubs, flowers, and grass.

These two aspects of wood represent wood that is growing or rising as it protrudes through the ground in the form of new shoots or young plants. Wood is an active energy.

The element of wood fuels the fire to make it burn.

YANG FIRE

This is a strong fire, the sun, power stations and electricity.

YIN FIRE

This is the fuel of the stove, central heating, lighting, and candlelight. Fire represents the height of the sun and the heat of the day. These two aspects represent the heat of fire in various degrees. When fire burns, it forms an ash that is then deposited on the earth.

The next forward element in the Five-Element Cycle is that of:

YANG EARTH

This is hard, dry earth, such as bricks that have been fired for construction.

YIN EARTH

This is the receiving earth that opens for the seed to be planted, then nurtures and encourages its growth. Mother Earth is Yin Earth; it produces the vegetation and guides the course of a river by forming the banks to give it direction.

Earth is a valuable element because it understands all other elements. Metal is born in the earth; metal can be anything precious such as bronze, silver, gold, diamonds, and jade.

The next forward element of the Five-Element Cycle is:

YANG METAL

This is raw metal, still buried in the ground. Its natural quality is to shine, but in its raw state it is buried in the earth and covered in soil. Yang Metal is solid and hard, and represents motorized vehicles, trains, planes, transmission towers, building structures, and weapons.

YIN METAL

This is soft metal that has been fired and crafted into something beautiful, such as a piece of jewelry or a watch.

Metal has two forms: solid and liquid. When solid metal is heated it becomes a liquid.

For this reason, the forward element in the Five-Element Cycle is:

YANG WATER

This is Heaven's water, rain, snow, hail, or a cloud that holds the water. Human sweat and steam are also Yang Water because they are rising. If you lose Yang Water, your skin becomes dry and you need to rehydrate.

YIN WATER

This is a reservoir of underground water, or drinking water that is above the ground. This water can be mixed with other things to produce something else, such as fruit juice, alcohol, and medicine.

Water is not an easy element to understand because it has no shape. When we look into a body of water, we have no concept of its depth. It may be very deep or it may be a puddle; on the surface, they look the same.

THE 10 HEAVENLY STEMS 天干

Heaven's Chi is represented by the 10 Heavenly Stems that each have a yin or yang aspect of one of the five elements.

THE 10 HEAVENLY STEMS

YANG WOOD	YIN WOOD		YANG FIRE	YIN FIRE
YANG EARTH	YIN EARTH		YANG METAL	YIN METAL
	YANG WATER	YIN WATER		

APPLYING THE 10 HEAVENLY STEMS TO OUR CHART

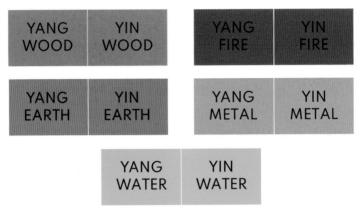

	TIME	DAY	MONTH	YEAR
	06:00	4th SELF	July	2022
HEAVEN STEMS	Yin Wood	Yang Earth	Yang Fire	Yang Water
EARTHLY BRANCHES	Yin Wood	Yang Fire	Yang Fire	Yang Wood

As discussed in the earlier part of this chapter, the Heavenly Stem present on the day of birth represents the self, in this case Yang Earth.

YANG EARTH

This is hard, dry earth, such as bricks that have been fired for construction. This person will therefore have a solid, reliable demeanor; building bricks carry a lot of responsibility.

Taking a further look at the relationship of the Heavenly Stems, we have Yang Water in the year pillar, Yin Wood in the time pillar and Yang Fire in the month pillar, all of which support the Yang Earth.

When a self-element has this sort of support, it indicates a strong-willed person—probably one with a stubborn streak, because the energy doesn't continue to flow from the self-element of earth to the forward element of metal.

12 EARTHLY BRANCHES 地支
REPRESENTING THE 12 ANIMALS OF THE CHINESE ZODIAC

Legend has it that the Lord Buddha summoned all the animals of his kingdom to his deathbed to bid them farewell. Just 12 animals made the journey, and in honor of their effort and commitment,

the Lord Buddha gave each animal a year in their name. The years were awarded in the order of their appearance at his bedside; hence the Cycle of the 12 Animals was born.

子	丑	寅	卯
RAT	**OX**	**TIGER**	**RABBIT**
YANG WATER	YIN EARTH	YANG WOOD	YIN WOOD

辰	巳	午	未
DRAGON	**SNAKE**	**HORSE**	**SHEEP**
YANG EARTH	YIN FIRE	YANG FIRE	YIN EARTH

申	酉	戌	亥
MONKEY	**ROOSTER**	**DOG**	**PIG**
YANG METAL	YIN METAL	YANG EARTH	YIN WATER

It was a long and arduous journey through the kingdom, the final section of which entailed crossing a fast-flowing river. The Rat knew the rapids were too strong for him so, noticing the mighty Ox lowering himself into the water, he quickly leapt onto the Ox's head and sailed across the river in comfort. On arriving at the far shore, the Rat quickly jumped onto dry land and rushed off to the Lord Buddha's home. Hence, he was the first to arrive, much to the disdain of the Ox.

YOUR YEAR OF BIRTH

The Chinese believe that a portion of the animal's character, according to your year of birth, will reside in your heart and resonate with your personality. Born in the year of the Rat, you will always be able to find solutions and a way out of challenging situations. The Rat is resilient, cunning, has a quick wit, and is highly astute. Born in the year of the Ox, you will be accommodating and empathetic, solid and reliable, happy with a slow and steady pace to life, and, of course, forgiving and not one to hold a grudge.

The following table identifies your animal according to your year of birth.

RAT	OX	TIGER	RABBIT	DRAGON	SNAKE
1924	1925	1926	1927	1928	1929
1936	1937	1938	1939	1940	1941
1948	1949	1950	1951	1952	1953
1960	1961	1962	1963	1964	1965
1972	1973	1974	1975	1976	1977
1984	1985	1986	1987	1988	1989
1996	1997	1998	1999	2000	2001
2008	2009	2010	2011	2012	2013
2020	2021	2022	2023	2024	2025

The color coding identifies the element of the Heavenly Stem that was present that year.

WATER	2022	A WATER TIGER YEAR
WOOD	2024	A WOODEN DRAGON YEAR
FIRE	2026	A FIRE HORSE YEAR
EARTH	2028	AN EARTH MONKEY YEAR
METAL	2030	A METAL DOG YEAR

HORSE	SHEEP	MONKEY	ROOSTER	DOG	PIG
1930	1931	1932	1933	1934	1935
1942	1943	1944	1945	1946	1947
1954	1955	1956	1957	1958	1959
1966	1967	1968	1969	1970	1971
1978	1979	1980	1981	1982	1983
1990	1991	1992	1993	1994	1995
2002	2003	2004	2005	2006	2007
2014	2015	2016	2017	2018	2019
2026	2027	2028	2029	2030	2031

Chapter 5

THE 12 ANIMALS OF THE CHINESE ZODIAC

P eople are natural followers, and are influenced by the nature of their surroundings. For example, in a surfing resort, with the buzz and activity of young people, the roar of the ocean, the smell of fish and chips, the music, and the laughter you are not going to sit quietly and read a book. The form is active, and therefore the people are active. Conversely, in a graveyard the form is quiet, and you would not dream of having a barbecue and playing loud music. Quiet form dictates a quiet activity. The following descriptions of the 12 animals of the Chinese zodiac illustrate the form of those animals, a form that anyone born in that year will naturally follow. The 12 animals therefore identify with the traits that are recognizable in you, according to your year of birth. It must be understood that there is no hierarchy; the animals are all part of the same family, and all have a different contribution to make. No animal is better or worse; they simply understand their strengths and their skills, and leave the jobs that don't suit them to someone who is happy to pick up the reins.

In this chapter, each animal's general characteristics are described, followed by a more specific view of the animal according to the impact of the element of the Heavenly Stem that it is sitting with in a given year. There are five different aspects of each animal:

For Example:
The Wood Tiger, the Fire Tiger, the Earth Tiger, the Metal Tiger, and the Water Tiger.

	TIME 06:00	DAY 4th	MONTH July	YEAR 2022
HEAVEN STEMS	Yin Wood	Yang Earth	Yang Fire	Yang Water
EARTHLY BRANCHES	Yin Wood	Yang Fire	Yang Fire	Yang Wood
HEAVEN/ EARTH	WOOD RABBIT	EARTH HORSE	FIRE HORSE	WATER TIGER

Our example can now have the 12 animals inserted into the chart.

Using the year pillar, born in 2022, we can see this is the year of the Tiger, but more specifically 2022 is the year of the Water Tiger because of the influence of the Heavenly Stem. To understand this aspect of the personality of this person is to understand the interaction of the two elements in this pillar. This interaction is of vital importance. In the Five-Element Cycle,

Water feeds Wood; therefore Heaven's will is supportive of the Tiger and will encourage it to succeed.

The Water Tiger has webbed feet and a natural ability to swim fast. It can move through the water at an exceptional speed, making it a formidable opponent when hunting fish for dinner. In 2022, it was therefore necessary to keep your eye on the target; if you hesitate, a competitor could seize the moment and grab the prize. Anyone born in this year will be ambitious and eager to learn.

THE RAT

THE ELEMENT OF WATER

Before the Han Dynasty 206BCE–220CE, the Rat month was the first month of the year.

After the Han Dynasty, the Tiger was set as the first month and the Rat came to represent the month of December, as the Rat is associated with the water element and this is abundant in December, with rain and snow.

The first to arrive at the Lord Buddha's bedside, the Rat leads the Cycle of the 12 Animals; understanding the importance of continuity, the Rat therefore represents new beginnings. He holds a major role of responsibility at the end of the year, as he is handing over the energy of the old year, which is very tired at this stage, onto the fragile and immature energy of the New Year. The Rat is a diplomat and a mediator that moves forward with enthusiasm in his attempt to provide a fresh start for all. It is interesting to note the problematic energy that occurs between one year ending and a new year starting in the months of December and January, when family harmony is often pushed to its limits and divorce rates soar. This is due to the mixed energy between the two years that causes instability. The Rat carries a huge weight of responsibility until he can hand over the energy to the next animal, the Ox; but his bravery prevails, as he always gives his all and does his best.

Rats are always close to people, as they only live where humans reside. For this reason, anyone born in the year of the Rat

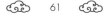

61

will have a high ability to adapt to, and live in, any environment. The dexterity of the Rat shows in his resolution of the problem of the Ox's superiority in strength and power as they journeyed together to the Lord Buddha's bedside. Never one to be beaten by a challenge, he will use all his resources to try to turn a difficult situation around. The Rat is a survivor with a very competitive streak. That makes him stand out in a crowd and affords him leadership qualities and an understanding of responsibility. He is also a very loyal family member, and will fight to defend his offspring as well as his own rights. He has a strong sense of right and wrong, although he is not averse to bending the rules when its suits him, as the Ox found out to his displeasure.

The Rat represents the element of Water and, like water, he finds it hard to be still. It is fair to say that the Rat is one to think on his feet; taking time out is not high on his agenda. The Rat is definitely not one to warm to restrictions; he likes his own rules and his own way of implementing them. Procrastination is not a word he uses. He is always thinking ahead, and of the next challenge, as he deals with the current job. He trusts very few people and finds delegation a hard pill to swallow as he believes the most reliable person in his life is himself. For this reason, he does not make a great team player, preferring an independent existence where he is free to use his own initiative and to come and go as he pleases.

The Chinese hold the Rat in high regard and respect his sensitivity. A sailor, for example, will not set sail on a ship with no rats on board, because he knows the Rat will always sense disaster; consequently the sailor will not risk his ship. In manufacturing, if rats move out of a factory building it is recognized as a warning that something is wrong, the likelihood being that a fire is coming. If a rat runs up a mountain it is because an earthquake is imminent, and if a water rat leaves the river, it is because a tsunami is building.

The Rat also represents the month of December. His role is to oversee the handover of the energy to the new year.

The Wood Rat—The Bamboo Rat
BORN 1924 / 1984 / 2044

The Wood Rat is happiest in nature, where he will find food from the roots contained in his underground burrow. He prefers a vegetarian diet, feeding mainly on the nuts and fruits of the forest. This Rat is particularly secretive, making it hard to see exactly where he is working. As a great climber, he can work above and below ground with ease.

He is very in tune with his environment; understanding the qualities of each season, he will plan his actions accordingly. He knows food will be scarce in the winter so, like the squirrel, he'll store food in the fall in preparation. He remembers the location of these stores because he has the added gift of a good memory. A Wood Rat person born in the fall will therefore usually live in a wealthy environment where there is plenty of food.

The Fire Rat—The City Rat
BORN 1936 / 1996 / 2056

The Fire Rat favors hot climates and city life. Food is not as plentiful for this Rat; he has to rely on all his resources to survive. He lives on his wit and ingenuity, and truly knows the meaning of dexterity and resilience to survive, because for him there are no guarantees. His temper can flare quickly too. It's not that he is aggressive; it's simply that he will do whatever it takes to provide

for his young, so he truly knows how to fight for survival. The Fire Rat loves the heat, and is at his most comfortable and confident if born in the summer.

The Earth Rat—The Field Rat
BORN 1948 / 2008 / 2068

The Earth Rat loves the great outdoors, preferring the hills and fields. He particularly dislikes the confines of the home. Having said that, he has great loyalty to his family, so when his day is done—and that's probably rather late in the day—he likes to return to the security of his home, where he can curl up with the support of his family. Despite his independence, he hates to sleep alone.

This Rat is the biggest and greediest of the five Rats, and his ambition knows no bounds, to the point where he can easily become a workaholic. He is at his most confident when born at the end of each season—in January, April, July, or October.

The Metal Rat—The Noisy Rat
BORN 1900 / 1960 / 2020

The Metal Rat is also like a squirrel, except he can't climb. He has a preference for city life due to his love of noise and activity, and he knows there's plenty of food there if he's prepared to scavenge for it. If this means being dishonest and cheeky, then so be it. He really doesn't see a problem. His approach is, "If a tree is laden with fruit, then what harm is there in taking a piece of that fruit from the tree? And who is going to miss it?" He tends to eat anything and everything, and does not restrict himself to a vegetarian diet. He is comfortable with people and holds no fear, but does tend to work at night with his preference for the cover

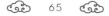

of darkness. All of this makes him flexible in adjusting to any circumstance; he's a problem-solver and a survivor.

The Metal Rat is at his most confident when born in the fall, and feels at his best when working with sound—for instance, in music or the arts.

The Water Rat—The Refined Rat
BORN 1912 / 1972 / 2032

The Water Rat lives in sewers or by a river, and does not feel comfortable if he is away from this damp environment. His preference is for the fresh water of canals and rivers; he has an aversion to saltwater. He tends to like cold weather rather than hot climates; ideally, he will make his home in the shade of a tree on the banks of a river. Unsurprisingly, he is a great swimmer and loves to eat fish when he can. This Rat truly knows what he wants and sets his standard high. He's not one to compromise himself. He likes quality and prides himself on his excellent taste and his penchant for fine dining.

The Water Rat is at his most comfortable when born in the winter, when the water is cold. Even though there are challenges in catching food, he can show off his skills and rise above them. For this reason, he embraces his reputation for endurance and fortitude in the water and makes a fantastic swimmer, diver or anything associated with endurance on water or in snow.

THE RAT'S TEAM

The Rat has a close relationship with the Ox, the Monkey, the Dragon, and the Pig. He is at odds with the energy of the Horse.

THE OX

THE ELEMENT OF EARTH

The Ox is a very spiritual animal, and very sensitive. Legend has it that humans can come back to earth as an Ox, as these animals are the next level down from humans. This particularly shows in agriculture, where the Ox works slowly and with determination, regardless of the hard work he encounters. He faces responsibilities with courage and completes each task step by step, despite the level of hardship. This makes the Ox totally reliable; ask him to do something, and he will complete the task to the best of his ability. His time frame may not match your expectations; he is slow and methodical, and usually gives deep thought to a project before embarking on it. The Ox eats in the same manner—slowly and methodically, chewing the cud many times, and with the same precision to get the most from his food.

The Ox likes to work hard and doesn't want a fancy life, so he's not very social. He prefers his own company—and he certainly doesn't rely on romantic relationships. In part, this is due to his inability to express himself. It's a challenge for him to explain how he feels to a partner. In truth, he is very reserved and private, so it's an absolute privilege if the Ox lets down his guard and allows you into his life. When this happens, the Ox makes a great friend, someone who is solid and reliable and will always be there for you in times of need. The Ox certainly prefers quality over quantity.

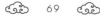

The Ox makes a great strategist due to his long consideration of any action. In the process, he looks at a scenario from every possible angle and devises a plan to cover all eventualities. For this reason, he is known for his straight-talking, systematic thinking and conservative ways. He is very much of the old school in manners and demeanor, and following fashion could not be further from his mind. A good pair of sturdy shoes is his only requirement. The Ox can be very successful in the property market, agriculture, trading, art, the performing arts, or medicine. He will hold his boss in high regard, and is a loyal and trusted employee.

Representing the element of Earth, the Ox certainly knows how to manage his neighbor, the Rat, and how to help calm the Rat's impulsive ways. In truth, he is a calm, rational strategist due to his methodical thinking, and is very happy in the financial world or accountancy. The Ox represents the month of January. His role is to control the flow of cold winter energy and protect the young shoots of spring.

The Wood Ox—The Forest Ox
BORN 1865 / 1925 / 1985

The Wood Ox is very much at one with nature, with a preference for country living, well away from city life. He tends to live in a herd, because that gives him a stronger sense of security and protection from potential predators. The Wood Ox loves farmland and takes great pride in his work, pulling the plow with strength and determination to do the job to the best of his ability. He is so committed and focused on the task at hand, he will forsake all else until the work is done. This animal lives to work because it is what he loves; it is his pleasure and his fulfillment.

The Fire Ox—The City Ox
BORN 1877 / 1937 / 1997

The Fire Ox is the type of Ox you will see living on the streets in India. Farmers often refer to this Ox as the bony Ox due to the fact that he finds it hard to gain weight; city life does not provide green pastures. In fact, the Fire Ox is greatly revered in Hindu culture because he is very spiritual and is thought to have a direct connection to Heaven. So anyone born in the year of the Fire Ox will be comfortable holding a position of high regard in the community, such as that of a priest or a Feng Shui master.

The Earth Ox—The Mountain Ox
BORN 1889 / 1949 / 2009

The Earth Ox is the most solid and reliable of the five types of Ox due to his love of the mountains from which he takes his strength. This Ox is totally at peace with nature and lives his life according to his rules: going to bed at dusk, rising at dawn, and roaming freely. He is his own man, and embraces his independence as a non-conformist. His hair may be long and his appearance unkempt, but those things are not important to him. To roam as a free spirit is his pleasure. The Earth Ox makes a good traveler, so working with a touring company of artists or musicians will suit him well.

The Metal Ox—The Bullfighter
BORN 1901 / 1961 / 2021

The Metal Ox is an honorable one who will always defend his honor both physically and verbally. It's not that he's naturally aggressive; it's more that he can't comprehend any sense of injustice, so he will always be a defender of the right. Playing

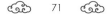

by the rules makes this Ox solid and reliable, and routine sits well with him. The female is always on time in the milking shed early in the morning because she knows this is her value and her responsibility. Maintaining a healthy diet is a high priority to this Ox, because he knows his value in the food chain. Someone born in this year will have a love of food and fine dining.

The Water Ox—The Buffalo
1913 / 1973 / 2033

The Water Buffalo is the most well-nourished and affluent of all oxen, making him the most successful in financial terms. One quality in attaining this wealth is his ability to adapt to different environments he may encounter in his quest for good fortune. So leaving the farmyard, if necessary, is an option for him. Having said that, he has an aversion to hot climates. This Ox should avoid gaining weight because it will not only compromise his health but also restrict his movements.

THE OX'S TEAM

The Ox gets along particularly well with the Rat, the Rooster, and the Snake. The Pig can also bring something to his team as long as the Rat is there too. The one animal that the Ox tries to avoid is the Sheep.

THE TIGER

THE ELEMENT OF WOOD

The Tiger is the king of the jungle, and responsibility sits comfortably on his shoulders. In this regard, he is well respected. His contemporaries trust his judgment and value his input. He is extensively experienced and wise, and knows his role to perfection—a role he will execute thoroughly and to the best of his ability.

The Tiger doesn't tolerate fools and is always cautious in who he trusts. He knows his qualities and his skills, but being taken for granted doesn't sit well with the Tiger. He needs to feel that the respect he shows to others is reciprocated, to avoid a feeling of injustice.

The Tiger can ponder a situation for a considerable time before he takes action. But once the pieces of the puzzle are in place, he acts swiftly and with complete commitment. His word is his bond and, once the commitment is there, he will see the project through to completion. In the same vein, the Tiger never regrets anything he says, because everything he does comes from an objective standpoint.

The Tiger's natural ability is to hunt. So even when his body appears motionless and resting, his eyes are alert and keen to notice any opportunity. His mind is constantly evaluating the options before him. His attention to detail is exemplary, and very little escapes his watchful eye, so much so that he ranks alongside

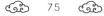

the eagle in the sharp-eye stakes. The eagle commands the view from the skies; the Tiger does so from the ground.

The Tiger has an insatiable appetite for achievement, and only rests when he knows his day has been well spent. There is no room for laziness; as soon as he has completed a project, he will move on to the next one. The Tiger changes jobs often throughout his career, because he has the constant feeling that he can expand his repertoire. Job hunting is a given skill of the Tiger.

For all the above reasons, the Tiger makes a good leader; he is brave, a risk-taker, and adventurous. This works well in industry and the military, but he can also work comfortably with the bad guy, the rebel, if he believes in his cause. Some would point an accusatory finger of single-mindedness and stubbornness his way, especially in matters of the heart, when his intense demeanor becomes overwhelming. Responsibility is only accepted when it suits his own needs.

The Tiger represents the month of February. His role is to encourage the growth of the young plants and vegetation of spring.

The Wood Tiger—The Forest Tiger
BORN 1914 / 1974 / 2034

The Wood Tiger is the most confident of the Tigers, and respects the value of his strong root, which gives him the ability to rise to any challenge. The Wood Tiger is a survivor. He is at one with nature and loves all things outdoors, where he finds rest and recuperation away from city life and the demands of the commercial world. This Tiger truly embraces his freedom. The Wood Tiger works well in education and industry. Leadership is his second name.

The Fire Tiger—The Ambitious Tiger
BORN 1926 / 1986 / 2046

The Tiger is known for his quick judgment and his ability to spot an opportunity—and the Fire Tiger is a forerunner in these skills. His eye is always on the target and on his progress, making him one of the most ambitious Tigers. He likes to learn new skills and will always take note of world affairs and market trends. He likes the activity of the city and the heat it presents—the buzz of the active yang energy and the hot motion of clubs and bars. This Tiger makes an excellent lover, as he particularly enjoys sex.

The Earth Tiger—The Conservative Tiger
BORN 1938 / 1998 / 2058

The Earth Tiger embraces his freedom, preferring life in the hills and mountains, and the calm of nature. This makes him a very conservative Tiger who is happy in his own space without the stress and demands of the commercial world. Leadership does not sit well with him. Living close to the natural world, he does understand the threat that a predator presents. His calm mind and acute senses serve him well in detecting vulnerabilities. He is a great strategist because he understands the value of knowing where the enemy is. You will never catch this Tiger off guard, as he loves the challenge of the unknown and he loves to make a fortune from danger; gambling sits well on his shoulders.

The Metal Tiger—The Thinker
BORN 1890 / 1950 / 2010

The Metal Tiger understands leadership and is not afraid to take responsibility in voicing an opinion. He likes to use his voice for public speaking or singing. He makes a good barrister, teacher, or actor—in fact, any profession associated with an audience. The Metal Tiger is a realist who doesn't trust easily, because he knows nothing in life comes free of charge. He has learned the hard way, through experience, and it may take time to earn his trust. Even then, it doesn't come easily, making him a Tiger with few close, valued friends and many associates that are kept at distance.

At first the Metal Tiger learns slowly; that is not a bad thing, as anything that builds slowly ensures a solid foundation and the longevity of the subject. From this reliable foundation he will progress quickly, as his logical mind is satisfied enough to trust the continuity of his studies. And that will enable him to go on to achieve great things. It might be said that his greatest failings are his overactive mind and his tendency to overthink things.

The Water Tiger—The Noble Tiger
BORN 1902 / 1962 / 2022

The Water Tiger is a confident one with an ability to make quick decisions and a quick getaway. Because his webbed feet make him formidable in the water, it is virtually impossible to catch this Tiger unaware. He makes an excellent fisherman and knows exactly when to cast his net. For him, food is plentiful, but this can lead to laziness on his part; hunting doesn't take a lot of effort, and thinking for himself becomes a rare occurrence. The frustration from this is apparent in his lack of application of his own abilities that lie dormant if he has enough food to eat. He likes the easy life.

THE TIGER'S TEAM

The Tiger works well with the Horse, the Dog, and the Pig, and is also in tune with the Rabbit and the Dragon—when they're together. The Tiger can't understand the energy of the Monkey.

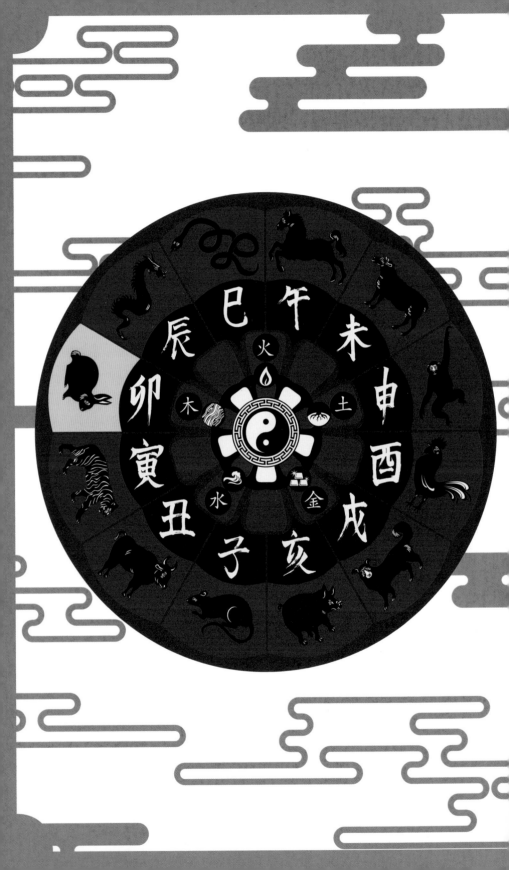

THE RABBIT

THE ELEMENT OF WOOD

Appearances count for a lot with the Rabbit, and he will always look coordinated and beautiful. The hair is well groomed, the skin or coat clean and radiant, and the nails manicured to perfection. The Rabbit believes in first impressions and plays to his own strengths to capitalize on that fact. He is a quiet and timid animal who understands his vulnerabilities. There are many predators in the forest, and he has great awareness of the value of the pack and the safety that numbers bring. He is very much a family man who is rarely seen standing alone. He possesses few weapons of defense—no sharp teeth or long claws—so the Rabbit rarely fights. He knows that his best strategy is to utilize his large feet and *run*.

Life for the Rabbit tends to be an even road with few ups and downs, seeing a steady progress made on his career path. He likes the sense of achievement and acclaim that success brings, but this will not be publicized; his modesty is more than satisfied in the achievement itself. He is a peaceful animal who is content with, and accepting of, his life. His love of the outdoors, as well as his love for all things relating to his home, are his priority. He takes pride in his home and is happy to provide a comfortable and secure sanctuary for his partner and their offspring. In this regard, the Rabbit makes an excellent interior designer or landscape gardener when he can apply his natural skills. As a team player, he will include his pack in all things, and shared responsibility will be taught by example. The Rabbit will not be averse to cooking the family dinner or sharing the housework. His caring nature knows no bounds, so working as a secretary, personal assistant, receptionist, host/hostess, or as a nurse will suit him.

The Rabbit represents the month of April. His role is to encourage the continuity and healthy growth of vegetation.

The Wooden Rabbit—The Forest Rabbit
BORN 1915 / 1975 / 2035

The Forest Rabbit is very much like the squirrel, who loves the natural environment, especially the forest, where he can be found climbing rocks and trees. Food is not as plentiful in the forest as the grazing grassland is rare. Never one to go hungry, however, he will dine on fallen fruits and the young roots of trees and shrubs. There are many predators in the forest that make the Wood Rabbit nervous and less sociable than other Rabbits; that disposition makes him prefer life at home, in the security of his burrow.

The Fire Rabbit—The Ambitious Rabbit
BORN 1927 / 1987 / 2047

The Fire Rabbit likes the heat. That's an unexpected characteristic for a creature that's already wearing a fur coat, but he knows how to use the intensity of the energy. This makes him streetwise, with a nonchalant attitude toward danger. The Fire Rabbit will rise to any challenge with a stoic nature. His best environment is in a hot country, since he knows how to survive. But caution is needed, because excessive heat can make him angry and prone to outbursts of temper.

The Earth Rabbit—The God Doctor
BORN 1939 / 1999 / 2059

The Earth Rabbit is a field Rabbit who is stubborn and conservative. He is happy with his life and doesn't expect more, making him unambitious. He is happy as the family pet; dinner is always provided, as is a warm and comfortable home. He can become accustomed to a high standard of living, and the vegetable garden is one of his favorite environments. He is a very honest Rabbit who values his good fortune. Chinese culture holds the Earth Rabbit in high regard, and he is sometimes addressed as the God Doctor, in reference to the example he sets in his eating habits, which are adapted when he is sick to cure his ailments.

The Metal Rabbit—The Hare
BORN 1951 / 2011 / 2071

The Metal Rabbit is a fighting Rabbit who very much likes to be the leader. He is comfortable in a position of authority and popular in his community; this bodes well with his love of music and socializing. He expects the best of everything: the best home, the best food, and invitations to the best parties. Having said that, he is an early riser; his favorite time of day is 7am to 9am, when the energy is rising and he can indulge himself in the fresh, dew-covered grass. This Rabbit does not shy away from responsibility. He makes a good boss who works well in industry due to his networking skills.

The Water Rabbit—The Otter
BORN 1903 / 1963 / 2023

This Rabbit is playful, much like the otter, who is at peace when surrounded by or immersing himself in a body of water. His favorite food is fresh fish, and he enjoys it more when it's shared with others; he loves to socialize and talk. Isolation does not always suit him. However, the water Rabbit can be comfortable alone, especially in the winter months. He is intelligent and diligent, working quietly at his studies until he achieves success in his exams—which he deserves. The Water Rabbit understands the value of balance.

THE RABBIT'S TEAM

The Rabbit works well with the Dog, the Pig, and the Sheep, and is happy to join in with the Tiger and the Dragon when they're together. The Rabbit does not enjoy the company of the Rooster.

THE DRAGON

THE ELEMENT OF EARTH

Dragon fossils have never been found, so he is the mythical creature of the 12 animals, who has a direct connection to Heaven's authority. He is held in high esteem in Chinese culture, and is said to attract auspicious opportunities in the workplace. To describe him as imaginative is an understatement; some of his ideas can seem extreme or unrealistic, making him an entrepreneur or inventor of great acclaim. However, such is his vivid imagination that he can be distracted by a new venture. This can make it hard for him to settle down at one job or one place. He is constantly climbing the career ladder, but will fluctuate between desiring a role of authority and working freelance so he can control his diary of commitments more easily. He is definitely his own man, and the female Dragon her own woman, forsaking family in the name of career gratification. The Dragon is well suited to a career in design, architecture, advertising, the arts, and cultural work.

Without a doubt, the Dragon carries tremendous qualities in leadership and commands huge respect from his fellow Chinese zodiac animals. His personal element is Earth, which all the other elements of the Five-Element Cycle rely on. The Wood of the tree needs the Earth to secure its roots, from which it gets nourishment. The Fire burns and forms ash that is deposited on the Earth. Metal is created in the Earth, and Water relies on the

Earth for direction, which is provided by the banks of the river. All the elements rely on Earth, and the Dragon understands that more than anyone, and uses this fact, making him formidable in his leadership skills. He has the reputation of being connected to the mystical Heaven as well as understanding the Earth, with Man being the third energy in the Heaven, Earth, and Human Chi that creates all things. The Dragon is a visionary with his sights set high on the ladder of ambition.

The Dragon represents the month of April. His role is to protect the energy of the spring and ensure a smooth handover, encouraging the continuity of energy to the next season: summer.

The Wood Dragon—The Dinosaur
BORN 1904 / 1964 / 2024

The Wood Dragon lives off the land, and vegetation. His wisdom knows no bounds, due to his ancient connection to nature and years of experience. He doesn't feel comfortable in the city, preferring the peace and quiet of the countryside. He doesn't like mechanical things and would not be comfortable working in the aviation or automobile industry.

The Fire Dragon—The Direct Dragon
BORN 1916 / 1976 / 2036

The Fire Dragon is a bad-tempered Dragon who finds it hard to control his anger. He can be his own worst enemy; he loves heat and warm climates, but they only serve to exaggerate the pressure. He has learned to channel his energy and will speak with a clear tongue. He does believe that honesty is the best policy, so he will not hesitate to say exactly what he thinks, regardless of any offense it may cause. He believes it's best to

know exactly where you stand and what needs to be dealt with, as opposed to softening the blow with empty promises.

The Earth Dragon—The Mountain Dragon
BORN 1928 / 1988 / 2048

The Earth Dragon is known for being stubborn, set in his ways, and of a conservative nature. He particularly values his freedom and will shy away from any restrictions or control. He loves the natural environment of the mountains and will avoid the city at all costs. He is a much slower Dragon than his contemporaries, with a slow, steady gait that cannot and will not be rushed. Set in his ways, he will always be an "early to bed and early to rise" type with a penchant for the simple life.

The Metal Dragon—The City Dragon
BORN 1940 / 2000 / 2060

The Metal Dragon is particularly ambitious, and craves control and leadership. He likes to use his voice, whether in a position of authority or in a musical sense. He loves to be on show, to be the center of attention and play to an audience. His voice can always be heard because he is highly opinionated in all aspects of life and not afraid to share his viewpoint. This makes him a very social Dragon who is often seen out enjoying the nightlife of the city, where he can continue his repertoire to his heart's desire.

The Water Dragon—The Secretive Dragon
BORN 1952 / 2012 / 2072

The Water Dragon is the most intelligent and most discerning of the five Dragons; he is very hard-working but he also knows when to say no. He is a good teacher who leads by his own exacting example, but he will also hold something back to draw on another day. The Water Dragon is great in the business world. He is adept at keeping his competitors guessing. He handles money well too, always keeping something hidden away to fall back on if the necessity arises.

THE DRAGON'S TEAM

The Monkey, the Rat, and the Rooster are close allies of the Dragon. The Tiger and the Rabbit also connect well with him when the three of them are together. The Dog is least suited to the energy of the Dragon.

THE SNAKE

THE ELEMENT OF FIRE

The Snake, also known as the small Dragon, carries the Dragon's qualities but to a lesser degree; ambition, leadership, and a spiritual connection are at the forefront of his mind. He represents the element of Yin Fire; it's not the strongest fire, but it can still boil water. This affords him the gift of a warm heart, making him popular with his contemporaries, and the life of the party. Being the most attractive of the 12 animals, the Snake is comfortable in his sexuality—especially the females, who are passionate about romantic relationships and will not hold back in using their wiles to attract a mate.

The movement of the Snake is evasive, leading to a tendency to pop in and out of your life, often at unexpected moments. This isn't a personal affront; it's just that the Snake is busy in his quest to satisfy his own ambitions. But rest assured, he will be watching from a distance, because he likes to stay ahead of the competition. This gives him the reputation of being cold and calculating to those who don't truly know him; his family and close friends say otherwise.

The warm-hearted Snake has many talents—notably that of a skilled communicator who would do well as a psychiatrist, counselor, therapist, priest, or nurse. A social animal, the Snake likes to be involved and hates to think he is missing anything—his main criterion is being in control. For this reason, he does tend to hunt alone, preferring to delegate rather than work as a team. He is a motivator and hard-working, but caution is needed, as he can easily change direction if he deems it necessary. Always remember that the Snake is a decision-maker, and he must be the best.

The Snake represents the month of May and the birth of warmer energy that nurtures and encourages the continuity and growth of that energy.

The Wood Snake—The Forest Snake
BORN 1905 / 1965 / 2025

The Wood Snake's main predator is the falcon, so the Forest Snake needs to be particularly careful of him. Luckily, Snakes are masters of disguise, with plenty of long grass to use as cover and with a command of their environment. This will manifest as a person who knows how to circulate in a social or networking situation, all the time with his eye on his target; he knows exactly who he intends to single out, and where he intends to pop up next.

The Fire Snake—The Poisonous Snake
BORN 1917 / 1977 / 2037

The natural inclination of the Snake is to creep out from under his cool rock and bask in the warm sunshine. This is particularly important to the Fire Snake if he wants to preserve his health; he has a major aversion to cold weather. In fact, fire energy is all he understands, making him active, social, and confident. He is fully committed to his own cause, and that can sometimes lead to him becoming a workaholic, forsaking all others in his quest to be the best. His weakness is overcommitment when the fire energy gets

too strong and anger erupts. That's when his bite is dangerous and venomous.

The Earth Snake—The Small Dragon
BORN 1929 / 1989 / 2049

The Earth Snake is the local boy who knows his environment and his district, and he knows it well. There is a saying that a great Dragon is no match for a local Snake, meaning local knowledge and experience counts for a lot, and that a local who is familiar with his environment is more than a match for a stranger of great ability. The Earth Snake is particularly cunning in this regard. He is eager to prove his worth in the eyes of his competitors and is never satisfied until he gets his way, making him a determined and formidable competitor.

The Metal Snake—The Rattlesnake
BORN 1941 / 2001 / 2061

The Metal Snake is particularly thrifty and will take great care in saving his hard-earned cash. He is also known for the quality and allure of his voice, making him a great salesman who can hold the attention of potential clients. It's fair to say that he doesn't suffer fools gladly; tolerance is not one of his greatest attributes, so don't be surprised if you find yourself on the receiving end of his sharp tongue if you cause offense.

The Water Snake—The River Snake
BORN 1953 / 2013 / 2073

The Water Snake needs to be wary of extremely cold temperatures, as he naturally feels more comfortable in the warm sun. Living by the river, he does like the tranquility of the cool, fresh environment, which supports his natural affinity for water. But he has to be cautious of overload and overcommitment. This Snake is easygoing and flexible due to his logical thinking. And his bite is rarely used if he is respected. This is a Snake that rules with gentle persuasion, not a venomous bite.

THE SNAKE'S TEAM

The Snake works well with the Rooster, the Ox, and the Monkey. The Horse and the Sheep are close allies when the three can work together. The Snake does not tolerate the energy of the Pig.

THE HORSE

THE ELEMENT OF FIRE

The Horse is a strong animal that carries his power in his hindquarters, neck, and head. He is at one with nature, and is never happier than when he is running at full pace, with no saddle, mane flowing in the wind. This is when he truly feels like a free spirit. He has a close relationship with humans, and works hard to support his master by using his strength in the field, with a plow, carrying a soldier to battle, or transporting goods. Such is his dedication and bravery, he is always ready to rise to a challenge, no matter how demanding it might be, as he trusts his inner strength. Man has needed to earn the respect of the Horse, training him until he accepts a saddle and reins. This has never been an easy task, but once a Horse connects to the word of his master, he will always listen. But this only comes when he trusts and respects him—and it is a respect that must be earned.

The Horse is highly intuitive and spiritual, and takes great pride in all he does. His preference is for independence; he finds it hard to ask for help and, although he recognizes the value of working in a team, his ultimate ally is himself. The Horse likes to do things his own way. He has a quiet curiosity about all things and is conversant in many subjects. So, along with his warmth and sense of humor, he is a popular presence in the workplace and in social gatherings. Love and passion are two emotions that dominate the life of the Horse, and they make him a loyal friend and family member. Pride is another of his attributes, and his courage knows no bounds, so he will see the positives in all challenges, and fight with confidence to find his way through them. He respects his master and works with him as a team; they complement each other's qualities and, when united, they can be formidable. Nothing compares to the elegance and dignity of the Horse; from his muzzle to the tip of his tail, all aspects shout gallantry and grandeur. The Horse is prone to overindulgence; an abundance of fresh grass could lead to health issues. In the workplace this could translate as a workaholic who finds it hard to say no.

The Horse represents the month of June and the height of the energy that supports vegetation in full bloom.

The Wood Horse—The Trojan Horse
BORN 1954 / 2014 / 2074

The Wood Horse is full of confidence. No mountain is too high for him to climb; he trusts his abilities 100%. This makes him highly independent, and one who plays by his own rules. His leadership qualities are a natural extension of himself, and it takes little training for him to learn them. However, he does have a secretive side; expect the unexpected from him.

The Fire Horse—The Fighting Horse
BORN 1906 / 1966 / 2026

The Fire Horse is one of the strongest of the five Horses because of a solid root that holds him firm in any storm. That root may show in the security of the family, the strength of his achievements or his confidence. However it manifests itself, it

fills him with self-belief and a zest for life. What you see is what you get with this Horse. He has fire in his belly, and nothing can deter him in the pursuit of his ambitions, which are many and varied. This Horse finds it hard to stand still. His vulnerability is in controlling his temper, which can flare as easily as his nostrils. Thinking before he speaks is not one of his qualities.

The Earth Horse—The Cart Horse
BORN 1918 / 1978 / 2038

The Earth Horse is a hard-working Horse that takes great pride in his abilities and all he can produce. He is highly motivated, and will complete any task asked of him. He lives on the land, usually on a farm; he likes country living, and the peace and tranquility of nature. His stately stature and slow gait make him an approachable and popular member of his farmyard family, who he relates to with ease. He is always the one with an empathetic ear and words of wisdom in times of need.

The Metal Horse—The Royal Horse
BORN 1930 / 1990 / 2050

The Metal Horse is a responsible Horse that very much understands the energy of the current era. The pace of life has increased dramatically in the last decade, and is continuing to

do so; the Metal Horse helps others gain perspective on the demands of our time. He understands leadership and is adept with finances. Both attributes come naturally to him, so he feels no need to shout about them. This Horse represents old money, and carries dignity and pride; he is happy to serve, as he enjoys the sense of occasion that comes with it. The Metal Horse is very happy with his life and envies no one.

The Water Horse—The Racehorse
BORN 1942 / 2002 / 2062

The Water Horse is a very gentle Horse with a happy disposition. But don't be fooled; he can easily reconnect to his natural spirit, running free with the wind when the opportunity arises. He enjoys the good life, a good home, great food, and the best staff to tend to his needs. He prefers quality over quantity, while at the same time appreciating the dedication and commitment that his arduous training demands. This is someone you will see at the gym early in the morning, or outdoors in all weather with his personal trainer in the name of commitment to his fitness regime. This Horse is a winner, and is never comfortable unless he does so.

THE HORSE'S TEAM

The Horse works well with the Sheep, the Tiger, and the Dog. The Snake is also an ally if the Sheep is also present on the team. The Horse least tolerates the energy of the Rat.

THE SHEEP

THE ELEMENT OF EARTH

The Sheep is the calmest and most tolerant of the 12 animals, with an acceptance of his circumstances and an ability to adjust accordingly. He never wastes energy attempting the impossible; he simply bides his time until circumstances change in his favor. No hillside is too steep in his quest to find food; he always focuses on what he needs, not on what it takes to achieve his goal. Trust, endurance, and willpower are his natural gifts. He is a social animal and a family man who prefers to be among his flock—all of whom trust and depend on him. His reliability and loyalty know no bounds, and his logical brain will always find a solution. This supports his reputation for being considerate, especially of others. He will always put others' needs before his own.

Undoubtedly, looks can be deceptive. One's first impression of the Sheep might be of someone with a quiet and soft disposition, but that could not be further from the truth once he unlocks the vitality that he possesses deep inside. The Sheep is adept at distancing himself on an emotional level, giving rise to a pragmatic analysis of a situation that is needed to accomplish the task at hand. In industry, he works well in positions of responsibility: a chief executive, diplomat, or any profession that requires organization, communication, and structure. His challenge is the 9 to 5 work day, and the confinements of an

office environment; he needs the freedom of the mountainside, which gives him more flexibility. The female Sheep is particularly attractive to the opposite sex, especially to those who share her love of nature. She makes a loyal and dedicated partner, but she does need care, attention, and the reassurance of compliments. Sheep are passionate and compassionate in their relationships, very loyal and dedicated. Material possessions are not high on their agenda; their needs are simple. It is not a case of a lack of ambition but more one of where his priorities lie and providing for his family is his focus. A weak spot of the Sheep is the tendency to be stubborn, indifferent, and occasionally lazy. All of these traits have the potential to lead the Sheep to become set in his ways. Caution is also needed when it comes to sugary snacks; temptation is hard to resist.

The Sheep represents the month of July, after the energy has reached its peak and begins to decline. The role of the Sheep is to contain the valuable energy of vegetation and store it in preparation for fall and winter.

The Wood Sheep—The Mountain Goat
BORN 1955 / 2015 / 2075

No mountain is too high for this sheep in his quest to find food. Food is his motivation in life, and navigating a steep hillside is a small price to pay. Risks and danger pale into insignificance, making him a first-class problem solver.

The Fire Sheep—The Sprinter
BORN 1907 / 1967 / 2027

The Fire Sheep is a confident fellow who is proud of his achievements. He is more like the African Springbok with his

sleek appearance and fast mannerisms making him quick to seize an opportunity in his focus to stay ahead of his competitors. This makes him an excellent networker as social skills are second nature to him. The Fire Sheep is the most ambitious of the Sheep family.

The Earth Sheep—The Farm Sheep
BORN 1919 / 1979 / 2039

The Earth Sheep has a smiling face and is the life of the party. His mind is broad; he's always open to new ideas. He could be likened to a sunny day, as he brings lightness to others' lives. His weakness is in overstretching himself; it's important for him to recognize this and to be aware of his limitations. He is a kind and empathetic soul, a good listener, and good counsel. Once again, he needs to recognize his limits and direct his advice to the wounded soldier—not the whole army.

The Metal Sheep—The Dapper Sheep
BORN 1931 / 1991 / 2051

The Metal Sheep is known for his intelligence and his enthusiasm in carrying a project to completion. He is highly ambitious, with a desire to shine and stand out above the rest. He has a sharp mind and knows his qualities, not least of which is his beautiful coat, which can be used for everything from chamois leather to wool yarn and fabric. This Sheep is enterprising, to say the least.

The Water Sheep—The Milking Sheep/Goat
BORN 1943 / 2003 / 2063

The Water Sheep is the wealthiest and most successful businessman of all the Sheep, as he produces a commodity that everyone wants. He is adept at recognizing an opportunity and grabbing it before it passes him by. He realizes that opportunities rarely present themselves more than once. This makes him shrewd in the commercial world, with a logical and methodical brain that naturally understands market trends.

THE SHEEP'S TEAM

The Sheep works well with the Horse, the Pig, and the Rabbit. He is great as a team with the Tiger and Dragon. The energy the Sheep warms to least is that of the Ox.

THE MONKEY

THE ELEMENT OF METAL

The Monkey makes a wise leader. His sharp mind knows exactly when it is safe to grab food, away from the eyes of predators. He is a shrewd character who considers all aspects of a project, making him a fantastic organizer and director of operations. He is creative, and his logical mind makes him a problem solver; he can see solutions to tricky situations at a glance. Architects and building inspectors may deliberate over a property redevelopment, but the Monkey can see a solution in the blink of an eye. Always busy, the Monkey carries social status, making him a great communicator and a popular and welcome member of his team.

In his younger years, he will win awards for his agility by ensuring that his performance is noticed due to the added verbal contributions he makes. This brings rewards and status to the Monkey, and sets his financial standing for the rest of his life, which he values and manages with precision. He takes nothing for granted, and everything is measured. His career is smooth, his health is good, and he has a great life. His challenge is to make time to rest; overload leads to irritation and frustration; there's room for improvement when it comes to controlling his temper. Undoubtedly, the Monkey brings a lot of happiness and knows how to have fun. But there's a ploy behind this: he wants

to get close to people to secure his position, and even though he is highly educated, he always wants to know more. The Monkey is an opportunist who pursues his career with success. His weak spot is his tendency to tell lies that fail him in the end, so he would be wise to address this bad habit.

The Monkey represents the month of August and the beginning of fall. It is the role of the lighthearted Monkey to add a shot of energy to the journey of the chi, as its strength is beginning to wane.

The Wooden Monkey—The Acrobat
BORN 1944 / 2004 / 2064

The Wooden Monkey is the lighthearted and carefree Monkey that likes to spend his time swinging through life from branch to branch. This makes him a natural high-flier in the business world. There is no hesitation with this Monkey, and certainly no looking back with regret. He's always focused on the path forward.

The Fire Monkey—The Noble Monkey
BORN 1956 / 2016 / 2076

This is a volatile type of energy, and one that can suddenly expand, indicating the potential to suddenly become famous. The Fire Monkey knows what he's doing. His brain is rational and he knows the difference between right and wrong. He is astute in his investments and has a sixth sense regarding when to invest and when to withdraw.

The Earth Monkey—The Confident Monkey
BORN 1908 / 1968 / 2028

The Earth Monkey is powerful and strong, like a gorilla that is totally at peace with his life and his surroundings. He trusts

what he has and takes pleasure in it. Life treats him well, and financial rewards come naturally to him. Some may think he's just lucky, because his achievements appear to happen with the greatest of ease.

The Metal Monkey—The Respected Monkey
BORN 1920 / 1970 / 2030

The Metal Monkey is not one you would want to offend or get on the wrong side of. To do so would be to encourage his rage. It doesn't show often, but when it does you won't miss it. He is strong in his energy and has a total belief in himself and his abilities, making him stand up for his values and defend what he sees as his rights. This Monkey commands respect both physically and mentally.

The Water Monkey—The River Monkey
BORN 1932 / 1992 / 2052

This Monkey resides on the banks of the river and naturally has an affinity with the energy of water. He likes to bathe, swim, and catch his food in the river; these help develop his strong relationship with and understanding of water—to the point where he can sense a change of weather from its movement. The Water Monkey is highly intuitive.

THE MONKEY'S TEAM

The Monkey works well with the Snake, the Rat, and the Dragon. He also works well as a team of three with the Rooster and the Dog. The animal least compatible with the Monkey's energy is the Tiger.

THE ROOSTER

THE METAL ELEMENT

The Rooster is the most verbal and highly opinionated of the 12 animals. He rises early to be ahead of his competitors and to uphold his responsibility to motivate everyone. He loves the early morning when he is at one with nature and the rising sun, when the environment is quiet and the energy easier to sense. Using this to his advantage, he is known for his foresight and his ability to predict changes in the weather and warn of potential danger. He struts around the farmyard with an air of authority, always well prepared and well organized; he hates to waste time. His mind is clear, and he expects everyone to have the same level of enthusiasm. Incompetence is not tolerated in any shape or form. The Rooster's mind races, always planning, always administering his instructions, always ahead of the game, so much so that his voice can't keep up with the momentum. Consequently he will often have a speech disorder. In truth, the Rooster overstates his position and often can't fulfill his promises. His plans may be unrealistic and somewhat exaggerated. Impatience and a lack of faith in others are two of his weaknesses.

The Rooster is a lovable character who embraces the fact that each dawn is the gift of a new day. He appreciates the fresh start and has no time to dwell on the misfortunes of the past. Nothing is ever a mistake to the Rooster, as he values lessons—even the uncomfortable ones—learned from experience. This love of life

drives him forward as a leader who leads from the front, and by example, and that makes him ready to seize new opportunities. The Rooster is a brave heart and a warrior, not a worrier. He is a confident, outgoing character who embraces knowledge that he believes will benefit the whole world. His voice is his sword. Roosters make excellent journalists.

The Rooster represents the month of September and the height of autumn. The energy of vegetation is now truly stored below ground, in roots, making it possible to prune trees without causing damage.

The Wood Rooster—The Pheasant
BORN 1945 / 2005 / 2065

The Wood Rooster is very handsome with his exquisite plumage; he always takes pride in his appearance. He believes, as a leader, that first impressions count, and he will always be dressed for the occasion. He is well liked, well loved, and appreciates admiring looks from those under his spell.

The Fire Rooster—The Turkey
BORN 1957 / 2017 / 2077

The Fire Rooster is not afraid to stand out in a crowd, and his somewhat strange ideas on style and accessories make him unique. He is not one to follow fashion trends, preferring to make his own statement and be his own man. His mind races ahead of the pack with the clarity and confidence of a visionary; his ambition knows no bounds. His weakness is overcommitment; it's vital for him to remember his golden rule—early to bed and early to rise—as late nights simply don't work for him.

The Earth Rooster—The Farm Chicken
BORN 1969 / 2029 / 2089

The Earth Rooster is the domestic, maternal Rooster who likes to watch over her young in the peace and tranquility of the farmyard. Life has a simple role for this Rooster; drive and ambition aren't so vital, for she is content with her existence. She appreciates the regularity of food supplied and the security of her home; they protect her and her family from predators. Her babies are her life. Her weakness is that she is preoccupied with her own world, and not streetwise. That makes her an easy target for anyone wanting to take advantage.

The Metal Rooster—The Fighting Cockerel
BORN 1921 / 1981 / 2041

The Metal Rooster is the most confident Rooster. His bravery knows no bounds; confrontation is a skill that makes him a first-class negotiator. He is not afraid to lead from the front when going into battle, as his voice can be heard above the mayhem that goes with the territory. Danger is not a threat he recognizes; he will do whatever it takes to fulfill his commitment. This Rooster is happy to hold a position of ultimate responsibility, such as an army general or chief of police.

The Water Rooster—The Seagull
BORN 1933 / 1993 / 2053

The Water Rooster is extremely forthright, and does whatever it takes to achieve his goal. He can be aggressive if that's what is needed for someone to appreciate his authority and give in to his demands. It's not that the Water Rooster is selfish; it's simply that he knows where his priorities lie—and he realizes that, ultimately, it's impossible to please everyone. In truth, he is only protecting his own.

THE ROOSTER'S TEAM

The Rooster works very well with the Snake, the Ox, and the Dragon. He is more than willing to work in a team of three with the Monkey and the Dog.

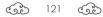

THE DOG

THE EARTH ELEMENT

The Dog is known as man's best friend, and one who will go to any length in the loyalty and duty stakes. To the Dog, it is an honor to be subservient, as there is no greater priority to him than commitment and reliability. Focus and hard work come naturally to him. The Dog is dedicated to his owner and is never happier than when he is by his side. Separation is not comfortable for him; he will worry about his owner's well-being until he returns. This makes the Dog a reliable employee who sits comfortably with responsibility and will see a job through to the best of his ability. His challenge is to stay calm in the face of adversity, as this can cause reason and rational thinking to fall by the wayside. When he can conquer this challenge, and learn to stay calm and keep an open mind, the Dog can rise to great heights in his career, using his qualities of sharp judgment and intuition. He is a worrier, and the most pessimistic of the 12 animals. Therefore, he needs encouragement to learn self-worth. He is, however, a good listener, and is willing to make sacrifices to win the trust of others as long as it doesn't jeopardize his integrity. In industry, he makes a good union leader, as he is happy to represent the minority. Because he is a good listener he makes a good priest, and since he's happy to work as a team or as an individual he is a respectful ally in a vice-chair position. The Dog embraces continuity, which makes him reluctant to change

and fond of the security of what he knows. This can be the case even when a circumstance is uncomfortable, for although the demands are high, he knows how to deal with them and doesn't trust the alternative that change can bring. In this respect, the Dog is his own worst enemy. He's not one to put himself first; he cares about the welfare of others more than his own. There is a saying: "A wise woman will fill her own cup first." In other words, if you are depleted, you have nothing with which to help others. This is a valuable mantra for the popular and charismatic Dog, who is always surrounded by admirers.

The Dog represents the month of October. The journey of the energy is below ground, the farmer has sown his seeds and it is the role of the Dog to keep the earth warm in preparation for winter.

The Wood Dog—The Guard Dog
BORN 1934 / 1994 / 2054

The Wood Dog has a keen sense of smell and is happy to use his gift in tracking, especially when working in nature. He is confident in his abilities and thoroughly enjoys the contribution he can make to the team. His wisdom and experience are evident, and nothing escapes his notice, for he has the eyes and senses of an eagle. The Wood Dog makes a great detective or bodyguard.

The Fire Dog—The Labrador
BORN 1946 / 2006 / 2066

There is no expectation too high in the eyes of the Fire Dog. He is 100% committed to his boss and is prepared to risk his life to serve him. This is a Dog who, when asked to do something, will carry out that task; it means a lot to him to see a job well done.

This shows the extent of his pride, and the service and support he can provide through his dedication to his boss. The Fire Dog is a first-class personal assistant.

The Earth Dog—The Sheep Dog
BORN 1958 / 2018 / 2078

The Earth Dog has an acute sense of justice and, as such, has a reputation as a defender of the first order. His alert nature and strong sixth sense keep him ahead of competitors; he gets ahead of the enemy by identifying the pitfalls before they show themselves. Such is his focus on his goal that others must clear the path to make way for this formidable force, who knows what he wants and how he is going to get it. Excuses are not part of his vocabulary. In truth, what you see is what you get with this guy: no frills, no airs, simply a genuine and sincere guy. The Earth Dog makes a good boss.

The Metal Dog—The Military Dog
BORN 1910 / 1970 / 2030

The Metal Dog is the gun dog, trained to retrieve. Also known as the Military Dog, he can be seen patrolling borders alongside law-enforcement officers in his quest to uphold his strong sense of right and wrong. Responsibility sits comfortably on his shoulders and pushes him to do a good job using his many resources, which leave no room for error. He is completely focused; nothing escapes his notice. In adverse situations such as natural disasters, it is the Metal Dog that leads from the front in the rescue operation. He pinpoints the areas where there is someone in need of help. This Dog is not a gambling man.

The Water Dog—The Banker

BORN 1922 / 1982 / 2042

The Water Dog knows how to handle his money, and might be accused of being frugal toward himself. But his generosity with others knows no bounds. The fact is, he's not money-motivated; he prefers love over money, although he does know how to take care of his money. He understands the commodity of money and its value. The Water Dog is a truly loyal Dog with a tremendous sense of family.

THE DOG'S TEAM

The Dog works well with the Rabbit, the Tiger, and the Horse. He will work well as a team of three with the Monkey and the Rooster. The Dog is totally opposed to the energy of the Dragon.

THE PIG

THE WATER ELEMENT

At the beginning of this chapter, I talked about the Rat, the first animal of the Chinese zodiac, and the responsibility this entails. The same can be said of the Pig. As the last of the 12 animals, he is a leader from the back. He holds responsibility for continuity in handing back the energy to the Rat for him to continue the next cycle. The Pig may look foolish, but don't be deceived. He has his eye on his responsibilities and, like all the other animals of the Chinese zodiac, will fulfill his role to the best of his ability. He understands the quality of a fresh new start and will see that the truth prevails before handing the energy over. Rest assured: there are no secrets with the Pig. So expect the unexpected, as nothing escapes his notice and nothing surpasses his sense of justice. He has a naturally sweet and sensitive nature and an understanding ear in times of need. He will always be ready to play the negotiator for a successful resolution. He knows no bounds in his commitment to handing over the purest aspect of a situation to ensure a solid new beginning.

The Pig is an excellent team player. Letting his side down is not a consideration. He is known for his solid and reliable demeanor and his sense of opportunity when there is a likelihood of him throwing caution to the wind, with no room for procrastination. The Pig knows what he wants, and he goes all out to get it. Some might call him greedy—and, in truth, the Pig does love his food.

But this quality only serves to manifest his insatiable appetite for business. He prefers to work in groups in which there is a hierarchy; the leader is easily identified because his tail is always up. This person will therefore be one to walk with confidence, his head held high, in his belief that he is a well-respected pillar of society. You will always know when he has entered the room, as he voices his strong opinions. He likes money, good food, and fine wine, but he's not good at managing these. He has a penchant for overindulgence. Having said that, he has no regrets; he will most certainly enjoy himself in the process.

The Pig represents the month of December, when he takes on the responsibilities outlined in the first paragraph.

The Wood Pig—The Wild Boar
BORN 1935 / 1995 / 2055

The Wood Pig carries an arrogance and a huge sense of importance, and likes to take control and assert his authority as master of all he surveys. He is often found residing on a mountain, in the shelter and protection of the forest, where he can catch his predators unaware as he uses the cover of vegetation. The Wood Pig is a realist that understands the dangers of his environment and the privilege of survival. He is a man of simple needs, is at one with nature, and is someone who will do whatever it takes to find a solution.

The Fire Pig—The Warthog
BORN 1947 / 2007 / 2067

The Fire Pig is a family man who prioritizes their well-being above all else. Nothing pleases him more than the sanctuary and support of his home. In this light, he is a provider, and always ensures that there's enough money to satisfy his family's needs. To him, family is everything, and even when a family member is in the wrong, he will defend them with his mantra: all for one and one for all.

The Earth Pig—The Farm Pig
BORN 1899 / 1959 / 2020

The Earth Pig is well provided for by the farmer, making him a Pig of few concerns who is happy in his world and doesn't crave anything more. This contented existence—with few responsibilities and few demands on his time—takes away any drive and ambition. He doesn't like to plan, preferring to live in the moment as his mood dictates. It is his lack of commitment that lets him down in relationships.

The Metal Pig—The Pot-Bellied Pig
BORN 1911 / 1971 / 2031

The Metal Pig likes the good life, much like his neighbor the Earth Pig. But this one is even more well cared for. His standards are high, and he will always choose quality over quantity. He's so confident, he will never contemplate failure—it's not an energy he has ever experienced. He understands status, achievement, and respect, and is also often blessed with family money or a position in the family firm. His vulnerability lies in taking too much for granted and lacking a fear of loss, which could result in a gambling habit.

The Water Pig—The Hippopotamus
BORN 1923 / 1983 / 2043

The Water Pig is full of confidence in his abilities and his strong root. That root may take the form of close family, a place he has known and loved all his life, or achievements and qualifications that keep him on the path of life. All will give him security when the challenges of life present themselves. This Pig's qualities and abilities know no bounds as it is impossible to gauge the depth of water—his element—by simply peering into it. This makes him a master at finding a solution.

THE PIG'S TEAM

The Pig works well with the Tiger, the Rabbit, and the Sheep. He is happy to join a team of three with the Rat and the Ox. The Pig has no connection to the Snake.

THE 12 ANIMALS, THE 12 MONTHS OF THE YEAR, AND THE 24 HOURS OF THE DAY

Each animal also has the responsibility of representing a certain month and a certain time of day. The following table illustrates the role of each animal.

The animal of the day is calculated according to a table, the 60-year cycle.

This cycle is based on the 10 Heavenly Stems and the 12 Earthly Branches and the possible permutations of the two energies that can be achieved before they are repeated. This is quite advanced, so for now we can take the information from a book, *The Ten Thousand Year Calendar*.

	ANIMAL	12 MONTHS	24 HOURS	CHARACTER
子	RAT	December	11pm–1am	The early riser with the cover of darkness
丑	OX	January	1am–3am	Chewing on his food and mulling things over
寅	TIGER	February	3am–5am	Perfect hunting time for the Tiger
卯	RABBIT	March	5am–7am	Eating the fresh dew-covered grass
辰	DRAGON	April	7am–9am	The entrepreneur keen to get to work
巳	SNAKE	May	9am–11am	Likes to feel the sun on his back
午	HORSE	June	11am–1pm	The height of the energy; horsepower
未	SHEEP	July	1pm–3pm	Grazing on the soft grass as the heat descends
申	MONKEY	August	3pm–5pm	A lively animal that helps keep the chi flowing
酉	ROOSTER	September	5pm–7pm	Heading to his roosting box for the night
戌	DOG	October	7pm–9pm	On guard as dusk sets in
亥	PIG	November	9pm–11pm	Time to wash away the grime of the day

CHAPTER

6

YOUR ENERGETIC DNA—BA ZI

THE 10,000 YEAR CALENDAR: THE CHINESE ASTROLOGY BIBLE

This book is based on both the lunar and the solar cycles and identifies the Heaven and Earth energies present in any given year, month, day, and hour. Its name is only a figurative one; the 10,000 years represent the continuity of the cycles of energy. Most calendars cover approximately 200 years.

The energies of a chart can be identified by reading the Chinese calligraphy relevant to the person's date of birth. The Heavens' impact on a chart is represented by the 10 Heavenly Stems and the Earth's energy by the 12 Earthly Branches.

This calendar can be purchased from Chinese bookstores. However, the only calendar available worldwide is based on the seasons of the Northern Hemisphere. After many years of intense research, my master, Grand Master Chan Kun Wah, has recognized that the Southern Hemisphere energies are different, and that the Northern Hemisphere calendar will give inaccuracies

when applied to people living in the Southern Hemisphere. The difference in the two hemispheres is easily illustrated if you observe water draining in a sink. In the Northern Hemisphere, the water drains clockwise, whereas in the Southern Hemisphere it drains counterclockwise.

	TIME 06:00	DAY 4th	MONTH July	YEAR 2022
HEAVENLY STEMS	Yin Wood	Yang Earth	Yang Fire	Yang Water
EARTHLY BRANCHES	Yin Wood	Yang Fire	Yang Fire	Yang Wood

After years of intense study and research, Grand Master Chan has produced his own 10,000-year calendar for use in the Southern Hemisphere; it is the only calendar of its kind available anywhere in the world. The subject of Chinese astrology is a very deep and intricate one, and it would be inappropriate, not to mention untimely, to convey the depths of this knowledge here. Suffice to say those born in the Southern Hemisphere need to take note of this fact.

Grand Master Chan is the wisest man I know; every aspect of Chinese astrology knowledge can be mapped into a person's life. His expertise comes from a long lineage of dedicated masters and from his personal research, application, and the evolution of his findings. He never gives a single piece of information without

facts to support his statements. This is the quality of Chue Style Feng Shui, and why we are simply the best in the field.

To learn to read the 10,000-year calendar is an art, and it takes dedication and practice to learn the calligraphy and the qualities the characters are representing.

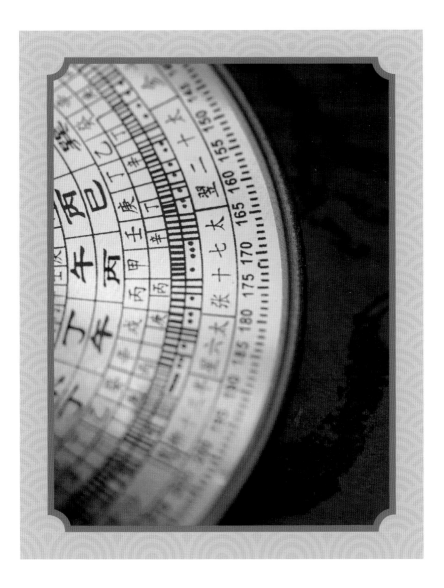

CHINESE NEW YEAR
is always the second new moon
after the winter solstice that was
in December of the previous year.

CHAPTER 7

WHAT'S IN IT FOR ME?

THE INFLUENCE OF THE FOUR PILLARS OF DESTINY ON YOUR LIFE

One of life's greatest gifts is the ability to follow the chi, for life is a rollercoaster ride with ups and downs, twists and turns. For some more than others, the path can have challenges. So when those times arise, a wise person doesn't try to change the unchangeable, but opts to follow the path being shown to them. This can take a leap of faith and trust in the universe that all is exactly right. And that can take a tremendous amount of courage.

For example: imagine that your college application has been unsuccessful, causing you to rethink your options and accept an offer from your second choice. While studying at that college, you meet someone who turns out to be the love of your life: your spouse, with whom you have children. Now you have a family. All of this came from trusting the process.

Following the chi means paying attention to the lessons being presented to you, lessons that are most likely not of your

choosing. It is the hardest lessons in life that bring the greatest progress. Naturally, we are emotional beings, and emotions can cloud our view. On such an occasion, the message is to sit tight, hold on, and wait for the calm to return. If there is an argumentative environment, fighting back will only add fuel to the fire of anger. Waiting for the storm to pass gives everyone time to gain perspective on the situation and allows an opportunity for a solution to emerge. This isn't a case of burying your head in the sand. It is more a case of taking a deep breath, and allowing time to calm the backlash and prevent a wounded animal from lashing out in desperation.

To understand the self through the eyes of your energetic DNA is to know your qualities and your limitations through nature's eyes. The characters of the Ba Zi have represented nature's stance in the cycles of life that impact you. Strengthening your qualities in times of need by following nature's direction makes you a formidable opponent who can show confidence in your decisions and accuracy in your actions.

CHAPTER
8

CASE
STUDIES

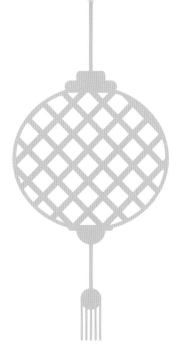

T aking a simplistic view of a birth chart, a case that immediately springs to mind is that of a young woman who had no idea of her purpose in life, especially regarding her career. She was 25 years old.

HOUR	DAY	MONTH	YEAR
YANG METAL	YANG METAL	YIN EARTH	YIN METAL
YANG EARTH	YANG WATER	YIN EARTH	YIN METAL

Her self-element is Yang Metal. This is raw metal, buried in the earth, waiting to be mined.

In the Five-Element Cycle, it is the element of Earth that supports Metal. So, seeing three aspects of Earth in her eight characters, it appears she is strong and well supported.

However, Yang Metal is raw metal that is still in the ground, so the three Earth elements only serve to bury this Yang Metal further beneath the surface. Metal's natural quality is to

shine and, with three aspects of Metal in the chart, it was clear that this young woman had gifts she could use. The challenge was to extract these qualities from the Earth.

In this chart, the Earth element represented parents and siblings. It turned out that she had come from a broken home, from a very young age, and that her parents and siblings had tried to support her ever since. In truth, she didn't know how to think for herself. Happily, once a flaw is identified it can transform and transmute with the help of the Five-Element Cycle. To support the transformation, I recommended the use of the Metal element to strengthen the self and gain some independence. This took the form of a course of acupuncture, as the needles are made of metal.

Metal that is lost in the ground needs encouragement to take a step into the unknown, because it has grown used to the security of its disguise. This can be achieved with the Wood element, because the roots of a tree can penetrate the Earth and break it up to facilitate the extraction of Metal. The bonus in the use of the Wood element is that it can absorb excess Water in the chart that could make the Earth element heavier and the Metal more difficult to extract.

In no time, I received a call from the young woman, who told me how much better she was feeling and how she'd noticed the amazing colors of the fall leaves. Her mother's reaction had been to tell her that the trees are this color every year—but this was the first time she had noticed them. The element that represents fall is Metal. This young woman went on to set up a successful business as a sports agent. Communication is a key factor in this field, and one that is represented by the element of Water. Water is the forward element of Metal—she had moved on.

This young man's self-element is Yin Water—a gentle and refreshing Water that likes to nourish. After graduating from college, he had set his sights on a career in central government, as a civil servant. He had received an invitation to a fast-track interview for an internship, and he asked me to support him in securing a job offer.

HOUR	DAY	MONTH	YEAR
YIN WATER	YIN WATER	YANG FIRE	YIN EARTH
YIN WATER	YIN EARTH	YANG FIRE	YIN EARTH

The year was 2022. This was the year of the Water Tiger—and Tigers represent Yang Wood.

The first challenge is that there is no Metal energy in the chart to offer support to his self-element of Yin Water. Luckily an added calculation can be made on the energy of the Life Path according to his current age of 25. In this case, he was sitting with the Monkey, which represents Yang Metal, so the support was there at that time, and therefore represented a window of opportunity.

His self-element of Yin Water is strong, with two aspects in the Heavenly Stems and one in the Earthly Branches, making him quite independent, self-reliant, and confident in his abilities. The challenge with this chart is the strength of the Fire element, as the Water can easily become boiling water, and evaporate. To strengthen him, I recommended the energy of the Rat,

representing Yang Water. In general terms, Water also represents communication.

The forward element of this chart is Wood and, although there is no immediate Wood element showing in the chart, the 2022 Tiger has brought in the Wood element.

The element of Wood is a rising energy; it grows, and is therefore associated with education and intelligence. The year was also creating a window of opportunity for him.

I deduced that he was strong enough to drive the career energy forward with the support of a Jade Rat and a strong pair of shoes. The shoe is the house of the foot, so wearing cheap shoes is like living in a poorly insulated home. Good shoes can also protect the brain, as all the nerve endings finish in the feet. In fact, when you hurt your feet you damage your brain, because the Heaven and Earth chi are disconnected. Of course, it is necessary to use the brain to further your career, making this a valuable recommendation.

This young man did not get the fast-track position. Instead, he received a better offer of a permanent position with the same employer.

It must be said that not all charts carry the same number of opportunities as these two examples. When advising on a chart, the aim of the consultant is to address an imbalance within the five elements to encourage a flow of energy through the chart, to free blockages and improve the client's quality of life. Chinese astrology is not a magic formula that can turn everyone into entrepreneurs. It works with a person's individuality. What it does do is identify strengths to build on and weaknesses to avoid.

T his chart belongs to a woman who was experiencing fertility issues and wanted to improve her chances of conception.

HOUR	DAY	MONTH	YEAR
YIN WOOD	YANG WOOD	YANG METAL	YANG WATER
YIN WATER	YANG FIRE	YANG EARTH	YANG WATER

Her self-element is Yang Wood. To conceive, the self-element—particularly in the case of the mother—needs to be strong. This chart is therefore looking at the Water element for support and, happily, there are three Water characters in this chart. The forward element of Wood is the Fire element, and represents the child as the element the self produces. There is one aspect of Fire in the chart, but its quality is reduced with three aspects of Water to control it. The irony is that the Water element is needed to support the mother but, like the young woman in the first example, who had too much of the Earth element burying her potential, this chart also needs to address the imbalance that the onslaught of the Water element is presenting to the Fire/child.

2019	The Earth Pig—Yin Water	The Water element continues to be strong.
2020	The Metal Rat—Yang Water	The Water element is even stronger because the Metal supports Water.
2021	The Metal Ox—Yin Earth	Yin Earth is wet Earth, and the Water energy continues to be a problem.
2022	The Water Tiger—Yang Wood	This is the best year to conceive, as the Water is feeding the Wood that can then produce the Fire/child.

These are simplistic views of charts designed to help your further your understanding. Chinese astrology can advise in all aspects of life, health, relationships, family harmony, finances, career, fertility, and even success on tests. It's all there in your energetic DNA.

BUILDING ON YOUR FOUNDATION

I trust that you have enjoyed the journey through these pages with me, and that your mind has been opened to the potential of a whole new world, which exists all around you. With this newfound freedom of choice, I hope you will feel more able to make informed decisions about your future, be it through continuing to study this fascinating subject, commissioning a birth chart or simply understanding more about the human connection to nature. and how we can help sustain our planet.

Chinese astrology is a Pandora's Box full of hidden treasures—and this is just the start of the journey. I hope I have showed you how Chinese astrology and Feng Shui work hand in hand, and helped you understand the energy of the 12 animals, and their impact on your home and workplace. Each member of this Zodiac family has its own seat around the 360 degrees of the compass, and brings its energy and characteristics to that space.

THE CIRCLE OF LIFE

There is nothing more comforting than the reassurance of the continuity of our routines. Naturally, we tire of routines at times, and yearn for a vacation. But it is with great vigor that children return to school after a long separation from their school friends, and the structure and stimulation of learning. Everything hinges on finding a true balance.

Routine brings reassurance. And that certainly has qualities that are brought about through the 360 degrees of the compass and the cycle of life according to the laws of nature.

ACKNOWLEDGEMENTS

The Chue Feng Shui Foundation Lineage, Great Grand Master Chue Yan Chan Kun Wah, the Chue Senior Masters, my students, and my fellow members of the Chue Yan generation of Chue Style Feng Shui.

With my love and very best wishes

MASTER KAY TOM CH DS YHH
THE ENERGY SPECIALIST

AUTHOR BIOGRAPHY

MASTER KAY TOM CH DS YHH

Kay Tom graduated as a Chue Style Feng Shui consultant in 1999 and was awarded the title of Master in Chinese Horoscope CH, Yuen Hom Hexagram Feng Shui YHH, and Auspicious Date Selection DS in 2006/2007 by her master, Grand Master Chan Kun Wah. She is passionate about her subject and travels worldwide from her base in the UK, in her endeavor to enhance the well-being and the quality of life of others through consulting in both the residential and commercial sectors.

Kay is a respected authority in her field, and writes extensively in a wide range of publications including the *Mail Online* and the *South China Morning Post* in Hong Kong. She is interviewed regularly on radio stations ranging from BBC Radio Leicester to stations around the world, Radio UK's Talk Radio, Radio New Zealand, and America's KRSO Radio in California. She is a teacher and public speaker, and has held the post of Chairman of the Chue Foundation for the last 20 years.

Grand Master Chan belongs to the Chue Yan generation of the Chue Feng Shui Lineage that dates to 960AD, the Song Dynasty, through the Imperial Courts of China. The unique quality of Chue is that all knowledge has been gained through the direct word of a master to his student, knowledge that has been previously extensively researched, making Chue Style Feng Shui second to none in both quality and validity.

FURTHER INFORMATION

Chue Feng Shui Foundation public newsletter with further insights into the potential of a birth chart: www.chuefoundation.org

Consultations and courses with Master Kay Tom CH DS YHH: www.theenergyspecialist.co.uk

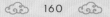